Self Sabotage

Overcome Self-sabotaging Behaviour for Life

(How to Be Nice to Yourself and Conquer Your Critical Inner Voice)

Mark Griffeth

Published By **Regina Loviusher**

Mark Griffeth

Self Sabotage: Overcome Self-sabotaging Behaviour for Life (How to Be Nice to Yourself and Conquer Your Critical Inner Voice)

ISBN 978-1-998901-19-7

No part of this guidebook shall be reproduced in any form without permission in writing from the publisher except in the case of brief quotations embodied in critical articles or reviews.

Legal & Disclaimer

The information contained in this ebook is not designed to replace or take the place of any form of medicine or professional medical advice. The information in this ebook has been provided for educational & entertainment purposes only.

The information contained in this book has been compiled from sources deemed reliable, and it is accurate to the best of the Author's knowledge; however, the Author cannot guarantee its accuracy and validity and cannot be held liable for any errors or omissions. Changes are periodically made to this book. You must consult your doctor or get professional medical advice before using any of the suggested remedies, techniques, or information in this book.

Upon using the information contained in this book, you agree to hold harmless the Author from and against any damages, costs, and expenses, including any legal fees potentially resulting from the application of any of the information provided by this guide. This disclaimer applies to any damages or injury caused by the use and application, whether directly or indirectly, of any advice or information presented, whether for breach of contract, tort, negligence, personal injury, criminal intent, or under any other cause of action.

You agree to accept all risks of using the information presented inside this book. You need to consult a professional medical practitioner in order to ensure you are both able and healthy enough to participate in this program.

Table Of Contents

Chapter 1: Compare Yourself To Others

"Don't be a slave to other people.

You lose confidence in youself.

Will Smith

How often do others compare you to yourself? How does this affect you? Many people feel ashamed when they compare themselves with others. This is because they believe they are not good enough or worthy of being compared to others. When you start comparing yourself to other people, you lose sight your own incredibleness. As confidence starts to fade, it becomes difficult to regain control. Remember that you are an individual and unique.

Everyone has a story to tell and it is important not to be able to compare your journey. Give yourself credit for all the achievements. One way to overcome this is to create a list with affirmations that you believe in and then say them aloud every day. You will start to feel better about yourself, and you will worry less about others.

Let's take another look at Peter's story.

Peter was a shy and timid person of short stature. Peter wanted to be a public speaker and he hoped that this would become his reality. But, his small stature, shyness, and inability to speak publicly made him feel less than he should have. He studied the great speakers who came before him and the people whom he respected, but his self-limiting beliefs about himself kept him from reaching the same level.

Peter felt that speakers he respected had a personality that was outgoing and they were also tall so others could see them. Peter lost confidence in himself due to this thinking. Peter's friends always complimented him for giving great advice, and sounding like a prolific speaker. Peter was happy inside. However, when he considered his mistakes, this feeling would leave him.

Peter got the chance to go to a live event with one his favorite speakers. During the speakers talk, he spoke about the dangers of comparing oneself with others and how it can affect individuals. Peter stood straight up to listen to the speaker. Peter began to think. He learned that people have flaws and should not compare themselves to others. He began to analyze his flaws and came up with ways to overcome his difficulties as a speaker.

Peter took what he heard from the speaker's presentation and started to apply it. Peter noticed a difference in his feelings about himself. He began to use positive affirmations throughout the day, and would switch any negative thoughts to positive. Peter's attitude and personality changed even noticed by his friends. Peter was happier, and his friends could sense the positive vibe he was experiencing in himself.

Peter took a second approach. He started to record videos and posted them on social networks. He started looking for speakers during his free hours and began comparing his own experiences to others in his talks. Peter is now the speaker he wanted to be. He has learned how to use his weaknesses to help others overcome theirs, so that they can live more positively.

It is important to remember, however, that no one is perfect. Everybody has flaws. To overcome these, you must not let them limit your ability to achieve your potential. Peter's story is an example of how Peter made his flaws work for him, so that he could be a powerful speaker.

It is easy to envy the success stories of others when we do not know what they went through. Some people had the courage to lose everything before reaching their highest point of success. Can you honestly say you would give everything up to become successful? Most people would say no.

Each of us have our own individual journey. Everyone who sets out to succeed will find their path. Change your enviousness toward others to admiration. You are not meant to imitate anyone, only God has created you that way. Do your best to improve yourself every day. Find ways to overcome your flaws and make them a part of your success.

You will find the examination on the following page. I encourage you to take the time to complete this exercise. This exercise can help you achieve your highest level of success.

EXAMINATION EXERCISE

1. What are some ways you have compared yourself to others

2. How has comparing yourself and others helped you?

3. What are the obstacles that keep you from achieving your goals?

4. What are some positive things you can do to motivate yourself towards success?

5. What are three habits you can use to help yourself stop comparing to others so that you can be your own person?

UNDERVALUING YOUR POTENTIAL

"We tend forget how far our journey has taken and just stay the same."

Realizing how little we have achieved.

~V.Jenkins

Are you one of those people who feel as though you haven't done enough in your life? Do you find it hard to take pride and be proud of yourself? Do you struggle with accepting compliments from others? If you answered "Yes" to these questions, you might struggle to see the value of yourself.

Everyone has witnessed some form of achievement in life. It doesn't matter if you are finishing highschool, getting the job that you always wanted, losing those extra pounds, or helping others in need. All of these activities add value and enrich your life. We tend to lose sight of how far we have come, and stay stuck. We tend to focus on the things we haven't done. This can make you feel worthless and unimportant because you are not where your potential is. Instead, look at every achievement as a step toward your goals. Instead, you become obsessed with your inadequacies and start to criticize others.

When we judge ourselves, it makes it difficult to accept compliments. Why? It is due to a lack in self-love, undervaluing ourselves and a tendency to assume that everyone else does as well. This manifests in our actions and towards others. Why? We treat others as we treat ourselves. A second reason why we shouldn't accept compliments is due to what we were taught at a young age. You can think about it for a second. Although you learned how to say "thanks" or to say nice words to others from your parents, they did not teach you how to get compliments back from others. The lack of knowledge in this important social skill leads to an inability to see the importance of it. It affects how you perceive yourself and affects the energy around you.

Mike was able withstand this kind of sabotaging behavior.

Mike was a professional with over 15 years' experience as a teacher. Mike knew from a young age that he wanted a career as a principal. However, he was very hard on his self when the idea of the next step came up. Although he knew that he had made a lot of progress as a teacher and principal, he felt out of reach. Mike always underestimated his potential. He was negative toward himself and refused to receive compliments from those who praise him for how good a teacher.

Mike was approached by a friend about the job openings that were soon to be created. Mike was the one he felt could do the job. Mike was charismatic, a leader, driven, and had a great relationship with students, parents, and teachers. Mike was asked about his position and said that he didn't believe he was a good teacher or principal candidate. However, a colleague recognized quality skills that would make Mike an ideal fit for the role, but Mike couldn't.

Mike reflected upon the conversation about the principal job that he had just finished with his colleague. Over the next few days, Mike dreamed of being in that role. Mike began to question his own abilities and was able to remember the many accomplishments of his years as an educator. Mike began to notice an increase in confidence as he started to realize the value he offered. A few days later, the principal position was posted. Mike submitted his resume immediately after which he was hired as principal for the following school year.

Mike wouldn't be able to make the transition from principal to teacher if he didn't recognize his value. Mike changed his life after that one conversation with a colleague. Sometimes, we need to be reminded of the potential that they see in us before we can recognize our own potential. After reading Mike's story, recognize the value you have in yourself.

It doesn't always have to be a huge accomplishment. We often overlook the small accomplishments. However, it is those small accomplishments that give us the ability to be grateful for greater achievements. Positive affirmations can be a great way to boost self-esteem and recognize your own worth. Write down positive affirmations to be posted on a mirror, or written in a diary. Then say those things daily. Accept compliments and be open to them. Start with a simple thank-you.

Here's a page that will help you recognize your potential and overcome undervaluing it, as Mike did. This will help you to get the answers you need.

EXAMINATION EXERCISE

1. List three things that you have done.

2. How did it make you feel to accomplish these things?

3. Next, go deeper. Now, stand in front a mirror. Take a look at yourself.

a. Name three things that you admire about yourself.

b. Then, go back to the beginning. Do the same exercise but this time, write down three internal qualities you enjoy about yourself.

4. Write a positive affirmation statement. This should be a positive affirmation that empowers you and strengthens your thought process.

EXAMINATION EXERCISE

1. Which limiting beliefs are you struggling to overcome?

2. How do you feel about these limiting beliefs?

3. These limiting beliefs are manifested in your daily actions.

4. It is important that you replace limiting beliefs with positive thinking. How can you change limiting beliefs?

5. Write an affirmation of purpose statement to change the limiting belief.

EXAMINATION EXERCISE

1. What problems do you face with time management

2. What is stopping you from completing your daily tasks or assignments?

3. How can we overcome the obstacles mentioned in question 2

4. How can you become a better manager and time manager today?

Chapter 2: Causes Of Negative Thoughts: How Did You Get There?

Do you ever feel a little too wrapped up in your own thoughts? Do you ever feel that your mind is constantly turning, recollecting, or thinking about things in a constant loop? Do you feel that your thoughts tend to be negative? You don't have to be negative if so, you can change your perspective. You must first understand what is causing all of these negative thoughts. Now that you have an understanding of the symptoms and causes of negative thinking, it is time for you to explore negative thoughts and the factors that lead to them.

There are many thoughts that we have in our heads each day. These thoughts may be either positive, or negative. How you deal with negative thoughts directly affects your happiness. Negative thoughts are something you can choose to ignore, accept, or confront. Whatever your choice, negative thoughts should be addressed. Negative thoughts can sap your life. These thoughts can lead to a decrease in self-confidence, self worth, and self-esteem. These thoughts can actually prevent you unlocking your true potential.

Past Experiences

It is possible that you may have done things in your history that you don't particularly proud of. These things could be embarrassing for you now. You may have done things differently than you planned. All the shame, embarrassment and guilt associated with past experiences can lead to negative thinking. These things may not be something you think about every day, but they are there from time to time. Two options are available to you when these things occur. You can choose to dwell on guilt or feel embarrassed. It is better to accept what happened, and then take steps to avoid it from bringing you down. Everyone makes mistakes.

Experience is the best teacher. No matter how many mistakes you made in the past don't let that dictate your present or future. It is possible to learn from your mistakes, but that's all. Nobody is perfect. Do not put on pressure to be perfect all time. I'm aware of the things that I have done in my past but they don't define my present or my future. I have acknowledged my past and learned from it. It is possible for you to do the same.

Learning from past mistakes is the best way for you to learn from them. Avoid repeating the same mistakes. If you feel embarrassed by something, you can look at it and decide what you will do differently if you have an opportunity to make the same or better choices. It is better to take the time to reflect, and not get down on yourself for the way things turned out. Once you have an answer, let it go. Learn from your mistakes and move forward to prevent the same thing from happening again. If you make the same mistakes repeatedly, that is a sign that your past has not taught you anything. Instead of beating yourself for the wrongs you have done, find ways to salvage the situation.

Your only failure is when your past mistakes are not learned from and you continue to make them. Negative thoughts often come from getting stuck in your past. Keep thinking about things that went wrong and you will not feel good about the current situation. Living in the past is a way to rob yourself of your future. You can regain control of your mind by accepting what you think. Recognize the existence of these thoughts, accept them and seek to understand their origins. It becomes much easier to solve any problem once you understand the cause. It's possible to be free of the past and live in the present.

Worrying About The Present

Many people worry about the past and future. Perhaps you are worried about your kids, work or family. Have you ever gone to work only to realize that you haven't locked your car or house properly? There are no need to worry about big issues. Even the smallest of issues can cause anxiety. Worry and fear can be interconnected. Fear that you might forget something can lead to worry. But it's just another manifestation of fear.

Information can be helpful. Information is helpful, but too much information can be harmful. Many people are constantly exposed to additional, sometimes useless, and sometimes even inexplicable information. It can be very difficult to grasp and remember essential information because of this excessive exposure to information. Fear of forgetting an important detail, combined with constant reminders about how others have missed out on opportunities due to forgetting it, can be a nagging problem. All of us live stressful lives with tight schedules. Because we are constantly on the run, forgetting to do something can easily eat away at our time. For example, if a task is not completed today, it will be due tomorrow. If that happens, you may not have enough time tomorrow to complete the tasks. It is OK if this happens every once in awhile. This is okay if it happens once in a while. If it keeps happening often, then you won't get anything done. To forget something today can prevent you from being at your best tomorrow. We all get stuck in a vicious loop of fear and forgetfulness. Fear of forgetting things causes fear.

It doesn't bother me when I see that I am losing ground. I like to be on top of everything at work. I feel disappointed if I don't do something. If this is you, it's time to break the vicious cycle. Fear breeds even more fear. So it's time to end fear and uncertainty. But how can you break out of this vicious cycle? The best way to combat this fear is to be organized. Make a routine for you and follow it. To keep your work organized, create a to do list. Make a list every night of all the tasks you have to do the next day before you go to bed. Set realistic, achievable, realistic, time-bound goals and specific measurable goals when you are setting these tasks. You'll be able to identify all tasks you must complete. This will help you to avoid forgetting important details or missing out on a good opportunity.

Eliminating anxiety can help you regain control over your life and allow you to think clearly. Fears of failure will decrease drastically. You can achieve your goals easier when you have control over your day. You no longer have that constant thought in your head that makes you wonder if something is missing. You can see all the things you need to complete on your to-dolist. It is important to organize your thoughts and actions in order to manage uncertainty and anxiety. Start delegating certain tasks from your to-do lists that you know can be accomplished by others. There is no requirement that you do everything alone. Recall that you are only human and may need to take a break from time-consuming tasks. Don't be embarrassed to delegate the work that you don't think is possible.

The Future is Scary

A lot of negative thinking stems often from one's fear for the future. If you are unsure of what is possible or what will happen, it's natural to be scared. Fearing the unknown has been a common trait for humankind. Since the dawning civilization, humans have been trying to predict their fate. Humans have been trying to predict their future for thousands of years. From our ancestors studying cracked turtle shells to identifying patterns in bird movement to throwing sticks onto the ground, to our modern ancestors, we have done so. The uncertainty of the future is what causes fear. You can create a plan of action and a strategy that will help you overcome any problems or failures. If you don't know the outcome, it is difficult to plan ahead. People worry about the unknown because they don't know what's coming next. Will their future bring them joy and happiness? Or will it bring with them a cloudy sky of doom?

Scientists have made it possible to predict certain outcomes within closed ecosystems, such as weather or elections. The average person is concerned about their future and often spends their time thinking about what might happen.

Some people are more optimistic and have high hopes for their future. There are also those who fear looking at the future. Many of these people worry about what the future holds. Most people think about their future. Planning for our future, envisioning our lives, planning for the future are all fine things. However, worrying about the future can make it difficult to remember your present. Do not waste your time, effort, or energy thinking about something that hasn't yet happened. This is akin to thinking that you are paying interest for a loan that hasn't been applied for.

Your future is not here at the moment. The fact that you cannot control your own future is what scares most people. Planning for the future can help you feel more in control. You can create your own blueprint and plan that you can use whenever you need. Set some goals before you begin planning. Begin by setting yourself long-term and shorter-term goals. Short-term goals should be able to help you reach your long term goals. For example, if your goal is to lose 50 lbs in 15 months then your short-term goal may be to exercise at least 3x per week and to lose at most three lbs per month.

Set goals that are specific, measurable. They should be attainable. Realistic. Time bound. If your goal doesn't fit any of these criteria you will only be disappointed. You need to be clear about what you want and how it can be achieved. Create a clear plan of action to set yourself up for success. Set a time limit so you can reach your goal. Without a time limit, it is more difficult to gauge your progress and increases procrastination. After setting goals for yourself, the next step in your journey is to develop a plan of attack.

If you don't have a plan for achieving your goal, it will be a wishful thinking. It is essential to have a step by step guide in order to achieve your goals. If you are interested, you could create a plan of action that covers the next few weeks or years. When creating a plan, make sure that there is some flexibility and you allow for some wiggle room. The future is unpredictable so don't make a plan that is rigid. There is no way to know what the future will bring. It is possible to reduce the uncertainty and ease anxiety by making plans. It is important to follow through with a plan. Knowing your goals and the way to get there will reduce uncertainty. Negative thoughts about the future are easily dispelled if you don't worry about it or aren't afraid of it. Plan for your future to combat negativity.

Your Habits

While it might seem absurd, the truth is that the more you think the harder it will be for you to stop thinking. Habits are the foundation of our existence. It becomes hard to get rid from a certain habit once you are used to it. The same holds true for your thoughts. The more time you put into thinking, the better you will think. Multitasking is something that most of us do. Your mind might be on one task, but your mind is on another. While you may be doing some housework, your mind is working on plans for the following week. Our brains are constantly analysing and evaluating things. It is tempting to spend too much time thinking. Overthinking not only wastes our time, it also drains our mental energy. Imagine that your spouse had an argument before you went to work the next morning. If you're prone to overthinking, this will result in your mind being fixed on the disagreement or argument from the morning. While you will physically be at work, you might make mistakes or be completely absorbed by the details of the day. Doing this will cause you to waste a lot mental energy, and reduce your productivity. These things can all lead to bad moods. If you feel negative about something, your brain will gravitate towards negativity.

Emotions

The majority of conscious thoughts we have are controlled by our emotions. When you are happy, your thoughts tend to be positive. If you're sad, your thoughts could be negative and pessimistic. If you notice that your thoughts are negative, it is time to take some time for yourself and find the root cause. Consider the emotions that you feel are worrying about the future. You may be worried about the future of your relationship due to disagreements that you had with your partner. These arguments could cause you to feel scared and anxious. The root cause of your anxiety and fear could be something you experienced in an earlier relationship. This could be with a friend, your family, or someone close to you. This fear is a trigger for negative thinking. It can be easier to overcome your fear once you have identified it. Do not try and change your emotion, or make excuses for it. You can just sit with it and learn from it. It is important to understand the root cause of the emotion. Acknowledge what you feel. Keep pushing it into a dark corner of the mind and it will eventually bubble up. If it does, it will likely bubble up and cause an emotional outburst.

Before you can alter your thoughts and beliefs, you must identify the causes. Identify the cause and resolve the issue. Do not ignore your thoughts. But, don't allow them or others to control you. Don't force anything on yourself. If you insist on something, you will be more resistant. Instead, make it a gradual learning process and an acceptance.

Chapter 3: Myths, Truths And Other Facts About

Procrastination

When it comes to procrastination, there are many thoughts that may be weighing on your mind. You might find it enjoyable to know you aren't the only one doing this, but there are things you must be aware of. While you could do research about procrastination, there are still truths to be found. These things go hand in hand, and it can be complicated to distinguish which is which.

These are the myths that procrastination is based on what you tell yourself whenever a task appears. Experts identified these myths as follows:

* Myth #1 Procrastination may be normal and even beneficial.

This myth is evidently based on the reality that humans are imperfect. This myth teaches that people can postpone things in order to gain a certain privilege. It's good for them, because it allows them to relax and "regroup", which can help them perform better later.

* Myth #2: Procrastination gives you a shot at being a better time manager.

Because you can't focus on effective time management when you're racing to meet a shorter deadline. This is a huge misinterpretation in the meaning of time management. Are you managing your time better? You are not managing your time better, this is obvious! You're not managing your time well by cramming.

* Myth #3, Procrastination can make you more productive under pressure

This myth is related to #2, as can be seen. This myth is easier to accept because it recognizes that people are capable of performing well under pressure. The problem is that not everyone can do this. The pressure of meeting short deadlines and extending time can make people break down and impact the quality of their work. There are other methods to improve your ability to work efficiently and effectively when under pressure. One thing is certain: procrastination does not belong in this category.

* Myth #4. Procrastination indicates that your motivation level isn't up to the task.

Many people who believe this myth say they need more motivation or time to finish a task. This is not true. No one requires such things in order to do their work. Just the fact that the task you are currently working on will remain a challenge tomorrow does not mean that it is worth delaying. You have the ability to make the task more enjoyable. It could be as simple and enjoyable as finishing ahead of others.

* Myth #5 (It is easy to overcome procrastination).

This belief will cause people to deviate occasionally from their work. They will tell you that they will only check their Facebook status, look at their email, or simply take a short nap, then return to work. Can you guess the next thing? These people will be more productive and have more work to do. It is very difficult to get rid of procrastination after it creeps in. While it might only take a minute to check your mailbox, once you have found some interesting information, it will make it difficult to return to work.

The myths above make it easy for people to think that procrastination cannot be taken lightly. You can end up ruining your life if it isn't dealt with. But how exactly can this happen? Consider these:

* Time is lost

* You won't miss the opportunities.

* Life goals cannot be achieved.

* Careers are at risk

* Self-esteem can go down.

* Weak decisions are inevitable

* Your reputation will be at great risk

* Stress-related health issues will set in.

These myths and truths about procrastination have been revealed. Now, you will be able to see why it is important to stop it from becoming a habit in your life. You can now take the first step to accomplish this in the next chapter. Learn more!

Chapter 4: Self-Improvement Work: 30 Days Challenge To Be The Best You

I'm going to start this segment by letting you know that positive thinking can actually change your brain. Think about all the memes you see everywhere, including on Facebook, Twitter Instagram, Tumblr and Instagram. Although they may sometimes be irritating, remember that anger is not like drinking poison and expecting someone to die. The more that an individual's thought patterns trend negative and slip into rumination-- continually turning over a situation in one's mind and focusing on its negative aspects--the easier it becomes to return automatically to these thought patterns. Ruminating can harm the neural structures responsible for emotions, memory and feelings. This is why the hell many of our lives are so unhealthy. To overcome our old self and get out of our ruts, let's learn to train our brains towards positivity, excitement, joy, and gratitude. You can forget about what you're not, and instead focus on what you are capable of and what you have been given. If you're ever in a situation that allows you to become self-aware, I urge you to think about what you would do if someone loved you. Sigmund Fréud defined libido "the energy, regarded a numerical magnitude... of the instincts which have something to do all that might be comprised under 'love. It is not love that is libido. I am speaking of unconditional love, appreciation, and gratitude. What would someone who unconditionally accepts their own worth do? It's so simple. But, it is also more complicated.

I see people becoming stuck in life a lot. We all have a past and cannot move on. This hinders performance, and can lead to problems in certain areas. It's because of our collective perception of the word "trauma", which can invoke painful false memories or true memories. It takes away our energy and causes us to think, "This may happen again." So we fear and plan for situations we don't want. We don't like to let go. It is easy to think that I cannot let this or that happen, but in my opinion, there are times when you can. I do not mean your past or that of the reader. I don't care if your past was bad, but I am referring to very serious ones. This could include a child rape, death in the family, any kind of grievances or abuse, as well as car accidents or years of hospitalization due to long-term health issues. All of this can be let go. It's possible. Because you think that your past will hold you back from having positive experiences, or limiting experiences in the future, it is best to let go. All of the things we hold onto in our heads are simply hang-ups. You should be aware of this. Even though it's just a memory, the past we keep reoccurring in our minds is still very real and vivid. This is what we are robbed of in our lives. The past is a concept. It is not true. The future is also not possible because it is only a projection of past events. We see things as we see them, not as the thing actually is. It was not an argument that you thought was a heated phone conversation with the telecom employee. The idea that you know everything about others is a hoax. You do not know their lives, no matter how much they may tell you. You can think of a traumatic past event that you would like to forget. After thinking about the incident, picture yourself living it again with all of the emotions and feelings that it brought up. The guided imagination exercise can help you let go of the past.

This should be done with your closed eyes. But, since you are reading this, you can also do the "closed eyed" version. Let your mind wander and focus on your breath. Keep your nose open at a normal pace. But, focus on the breath. Then, move your mouth out at your regular pace. Continue to do this. You can then, whilst still paying attention to your breathing, pay more attention to your body and how it feels. Notice how your stomach feels when you are sitting on a stool or in another position. You can keep focusing on this. Once you feel fully in control of your body, think this thought: "You do not have a future." "The future cannot be predicted." "You are 100% present now. The past is a myth. Now imagine it never happened. It is a myth that the past has never happened. How you feel, what you see, how you think, and what you can see through your closed eyes. It's all real. It is all happening now. It is important to take that in. Don't think about this. You can just be there now. Although you might feel cynical thinking that "the past isn't real as where I am now" but still feeling it, there may be other options that work for you. I am not Morpheus of "The Matrix", the blue pill that will end this story. Instead, you can lie in bed and believe anything you like. It is important to realize that your main reason for bringing up these events in your head over and over again is because you allow yourself time to drift from the present moment.

You can repeat the following after me. "I believe, therefore I am." This is how far-fetched this first idea goes. What is a thought anyway? And what about awareness? Let's be patient. We think in terms words, symbols, calculation, and images. Many of our thoughts, perceptions, beliefs and beliefs make reality possible. What happens if you see the unravelling web of beliefs falling before you?

It will be that you program your mind so you question everything you think about reality. Your emotions will be able to work with reality, and you will accept it as is. This includes science and religion as well as money, social systems, the brain, body, upbringing, life purpose and society. You can bet it's being questioned. Rethink reality. There is a chance that you are creating reality by narrating it with words. Reality exists independent from thought. Anybody's thought.

Let's say awareness. Most people think they are aware. We are conscious of rational constructs and labels as well images and emotions. This awareness is based on a basic state. If I took a pen and drew a sketch of a wall socket, it would just be in front of me. It happens that the illustration includes a picture, or maybe an internet emoticon, of a face. What would have originally occurred to your awareness?

First, it might seem that it is only the top of a socket wall, since that was the original drawing. But then, you might add, "No. It's the face. It is apparent that the emoticon lies right in middle of the photo." Or you might say, "It is both face and part of the socket." It is neither.

If we want to crack any code or awareness and reach many stages of awareness, then we must see the whole illustration in its entirety, without our minds projecting onto it.

You, the reader, are my concern. I will try to communicate to you subtlety as best as possible. To provide for you a guideline, a 30-day mapping of territory to help your become the best version you can be. I can't force any behavior except for raising your awareness and self-awareness. The basics of self-awareness are possible by reminding oneself, "I'm eating, I'm breathing, I'm talking, etc." throughout each day. All of it is up to your discretion. There is no guarantee that I will move you or inspire to take action psychologically.

Before I start my edification with this book I must first establish the path this book will follow. I've mentioned earlier, Abraham Maslow, and his term 'Self-Actualization'. This was derived directly from his famous

"Hierarchy of Needs", an introductory Psychology 101 course. The Hierarchy of Five Stages of the Hierarchy of Necessities is composed of Safety Needs, Psychological and Physiological (Basic), Love and Passion Needs, Safety Needs as well as Esteem Needs which should be regularly reviewed and Self-Actualization. This Occam's Razor approach, which is almost Occam's Razor, will be my catalyst for every series in the book. I will begin at beginner, then move to intermediate and then to mastery.

Chapter 5: Goals

We are now going to start with the topic "How do you set goals?" and other related ideas. Don't you have goals in your life? You most certainly do. You can probably list at least half dozen goals right now. Let me tell you, you may be working towards self-development. You might find that your positive mental behavior and patterns are improving. Your relationship with your boss or partner, your friends or your child/children could be improving.

Here's the thing though: most people don't actually have goals. They have goals they wish to achieve but are not able to realize. Real goals look like this:

* Specific.

They should be very clear. They should sound something like this: "I want start a company within 6 months to a full year in video game marketing." Or, "I'd like to homeschool my kids, because I have specific teachings to help them in life."

* The goal must be great.

It is possible to lose 5lbs and not lose it. Or, you can lose 50 pounds and still lose it. The greatest problem is complacency. Our brains like excremental goals. It's possible that losing 50lbs and continuing to lose it is easier than losing 5lbs and maintaining it.

* They must be written down.

It doesn't matter if you only have it in your head. This is particularly true for goals 5 years out. If your goal has a high level of significance, you can't simply write it down and then put it in a drawer. You have to keep up with it.

* Review your goal every single day.

It is a good idea to meditate for at least 30 minutes in the morning. Relax and just keep your intention in mind. Let your thoughts and emotions flow without resistance. How do you plan to achieve it? For every day.

* Your highest value must be aligned to your goal.

These goals won't be grounded if they are just random ideas from your family, friends, and extended family. You will find no place to stand on these goals. Your highest values must be written down and you should be specific. These should be reviewed and refined as needed. Next, set yourself strong ambitions and work towards achieving your goals. You can't only dream or think about it. Don't live in a world of fantasy. Talking about "shoulda", would-a. could-a. didn't." No, get out there and make it happen.

You should also remember that you can still succeed if your goals fail. It's okay if your goal fails. You can put it on the back burner. It is no longer important. This will allow you to touch on the priority. So you can see where you want to go.

Let's now look at the different ways that you can affectively set your goals. Let me introduce you to an important area of insight. This will enable you to have better psychological behaviors and routines, which will in turn open up new doors for your finances, your relationships, your family, and your personal growth towards a more fulfilled life. This is a common concept, yet it's often forgotten. It is judgment. Our reptilian brain has evolved over thousands to simultaneously develop its judgment mechanism. It is an area where the mind serves survival functions. This could also be called "fight or flight mechanism." Darwinian evolutionary thought socialized the notion of "survival by the fittest." Socialization refers to the process of each individual inheriting and forming the habits and skills necessary to be a part of their own society. Judgment is a slightly dysfunctional act that evolutionarily has been accepted as an acceptable part of modern culture.

The problem is that, although we evolved our rationality from hunting and gathering eras, it would have been impossible for us to judge a situation in which a tiger was approaching us. We couldn't process emotions like fear or fight so we could only use our judgement. Judging is an inherently miserable activity. As children, we subconsciously judge the people and places around us. By doing this, we divide an unbroken reality into 'good' and bad'. We are saying, "This is useful to us" and, "This is not helpful to us." Reality is all that it is. It remains neutral. It has always been and will continue being neutral. You might say, "Oh, well, reality doesn't have terrible things, like murder or genocide. Then are you saying that murder/genocide or suicide is not bad?" It's neutral?" I would reply, "These are events that exist in reality. I believe that at the moment, I do not have any suppressed and non-suppressed projections of the event. I can train myself to look at the whole of an event or set of events without giving it any meaning. When judgment comes up, you should identify it as a judgement. Next, ask yourself the following questions: "Is it a judgment that has brought up in me?" "When I recite what the judgment is, where do my feelings of discomfort?

We have a general sense for resonance with our own species. If you're just starting to develop your personal skills, you will gravitate away form 'toxic' people towards people that remind you of yourself. Ask yourself the following questions: Who in my life will just lead me down a road I don't want? Don't listen to people that constantly criticize and complain.

You will start to notice the traits you dislike in people around you. This is precisely why critics are so well matched with others who are critical. The magnets acting as magnets are the north and southern poles. Because of rotation on the earth's axis, the poles are not separated. It's interconnected because of the centrifugal force, and all its variables. This shows me that we are all connected. It is said that like attracts like. It's easy to attract people with toxic self-reporting and others who are grounded. Your sponge-y nature may make you too spongy. You can absorb the experiences of others. Nothing can give you more than you can give. Try imagining your self as a tree. (This is a contemplation exercise). Every inhale will be the roots of your feet pushing out from the ground. And as you exhale, the roots sink deeper into ground. Breathe in, hold it for 4 seconds, then breathe out, holding for 4 second. This is an excellent grounding exercise. Carl Rogers put it well: "The degree in which I can create relationships which facilitate growth of others separately is a measurement of the growth that I have achieved within myself." This is top-notch wisdom to bring forth. While intelligence is the ability to know others, wisdom is the ability to know oneself.

You can recite this phrase in your mind: "Simply, gentle." You can relax and let it go. Remind yourself of that throughout your days. There are two things that can make you a workaholic: fantasy and feeling like you're being blown away by the wind. You won't be able to see the Milky Way Galaxies from your perspective if you don't think. It is easy to become neurotic when we have so much data at our disposal. Addictions can be described as: over-eating; drugs and alcohol; masturbation; sex; shopping; television and the internet. How would you react if I told that you can become highly addicted to working? The collective human experience of happiness is not the same as true happiness. All emotions should be examined and personalised. We mean happiness when we refer to excitement. Imagine taking a spectacular shot of a family bees pollinating high-heeled flowers.

It could be kept in your home as a reminder about a happy moment in your life. You could also imagine that you took the picture together and that a friend of yours bought a copy. You'd feel excited, and everyone around would too. This is the way work should be. If you are a workaholic, it is likely that there is something deeper. Perhaps your father, mother, or caretaker often invalidated negative or positive emotions as a child. This causes a disconnect between us emotionally and our feelings, particularly in men. We are all taught to be left-brained.

Not what I am advocating is being lazy. To cultivate a state of detachment, this is what I am recommending. You will start to notice, paradoxically, that this can help you become more motivated and have more clarity. Your life purpose or your search for that purpose will inspire and motivate you. You will be inspired by your life purpose or the search for it. Your subconscious mind will naturally rewire itself over time. This will help you to start to do the things that are important to you. There is no catch. It's you who will naturally say, "I am going to fifing do it!" Most importantly, I will naturally see myself projecting cheats or shortcuts. You can program your mind with new patterns and it will naturally follow them.

Motivation is the subject of much discussion. Inspiration is a better idea. It holds a greater linguistic force. But motivation is the most important ingredient. There are two types. Both positive and negatively motivated people exist. What is negative motiv? You probably do it subconsciously or unconsciously. You want to accomplish something, but the part of yourself that seeks greatness is in conflict with your scoundrel side.

Chapter 6: How To Convince People To Say Yes And To Want You To Win

Persuasion can be a powerful tool when you are trying win something. It is possible to persuade people to agree to your terms in any situation. It is possible to persuade people to agree to your request even when they aren't ready to. If you make people want you to win, they will be more likely to support you. Although it can be difficult, convincing your opponent to allow you to win is possible.

Not all convincing others involves getting down on your knees, begging and trying to convince them. It only makes your character weaker and more stupid. It's about appealing to peoples' egos in order to get them to like you and want your help. People should feel like they can help you, and you must make them like you.

Turn a No into a Yes

Permission from people is essential if you are to achieve your goals in life. The keys to what you desire are held by some people. Sometimes it is enough to ask nicely. Sometimes, asking nicely is not enough.

The principle of reciprocity, which is the first principle behind persuasion, is what we call it. This is where you can make someone owe something to you. You do something to someone and they have to repay you. It is possible to save favors for when you really need them. Don't be afraid to ask for favors.

Persuasion can also be made more effective by being intimidating. You will make people feel like you have the right idea and they will be scared to say no. They will instead say yes. Although you should avoid making threats, you can use things like blackmail and sternness to force people to accept your intimidation tactics. If you are serious about your business, they will be more likely to let you take their side.

When trying to convince someone to say yes, emphasize the benefits to them. It's not about you and your desires. No one cares about your wishes. People are only out to make themselves happy. Give them some incentive to help. Sometimes, all someone needs to be motivated is ego-stroking. If they do what you ask, they will feel happier about themselves.

It can help you get ahead when you are well-liked. You will have more influence if you are liked by others. Popularity will make other people want to be friends with you. Be warm, caring and charismatic. Be sure to make friends at high levels and be wise about choosing who you associate. If you are surrounded by influential, good friends, you will receive more support and be able to do the things you want.

Encourage people to like and support you

People will be more inclined to support you if they like you. If they like you, they will do their best to help. A great confidence booster is having others rooting for your success.

It's not difficult to make people like you. Finding common ground with people is all that's required to make them feel understood. If you can find common ground, it creates a bond. It's easy to be friendly with co-workers by complaining about the work they do.

Friends can be earned by being kind and thoughtful. Remember birthdays. Always be open to new opportunities. Keep them smiling by having something positive to say and a big smile. You should compliment others - and do so with sincerity. Flattery only works if it is sincere. If you can make people feel that you care about them and that they are loved, it will touch their egos. You make them feel good and they will want to keep you around.

You can get people to think differently about their positions

If someone tells your no, it is important to make him change his mind. Show him how you are losing or missing out by not giving what you want. You can show him the benefits that he'll get if he makes a change of mind.

It is possible to use convincing arguments and hard evidence to prove that someone is wrong. Do it with grace and courtesy. Nobody likes being told they are wrong. You can simply show the person the error of their thinking and then present the evidence to prove it. Don't give condescending speeches or exaggerate how right you were all along. You will only make this person more angry and make him think twice.

Sometimes, however they won't change their mind or even say yes. If this happens, it's time to quit. Try moving on, regardless of whether he is present. Find another way to get the results you desire that doesn't involve him. Show the world that it doesn't take permission for you to get what you want.

Earn favor with your Opponent

You can win any game you play in life by earning the favor of your opponent. If you do this, your opponent will agree to let it win. This can happen in a number of ways.

You can win his sympathy by doing so. Let him see that you have gone through many trials and tribulations. Let him know if he has lost someone dear or suffered from a horrible event in his life. Let's say he lost his father due to cancer. You could also tell him that you have lost your father to the same illness. This will make him more like you and help you feel even worse.

You can also gain favor by doing something for your opponent. Make it seem like you're his best friend. Then, he might reconsider decimating and you. However, this does not always work because some people are self-serving. They will often turn their backs against friends. However, if your goal is to win his heart, it will be easier. Make yourself seem like a great person and make an effort to get along with him.

If you can offer your opponent something that is truly important, you can gain favor. You might be friends with a woman he likes. He will soon realize that if he lets you have your way, it can make him more friendly so you can introduce them both. To earn concessions from him, you need to find out his true desires and offer them your best.

You can have favor with him even if you are scared of him. If he knows you have the power over him, like his job or his marriage then he will give you his full support. Being able to control someone is priceless. Find any way to get power over someone to make them fall for you and to please.

It is up to you. Figure out how badly your injuries are. Next, figure out how damage control can help you get back on your feet.

If you're really clever, you could even use a blow by your enemy as a way for you to gain. Playing the victim can make others feel sorry for you, and encourage them to turn against the other side. He is a terrible person, so expose his tricks. You could also show your humanity and willingness to accept the suffering of others to make yourself more likable and approachable. This dirt can be used to gain likes by the minority if your opponent exposes any dirt about you or your past. Let people know that you aren't only vulnerable, but also unique.

Chapter 7: Living Happily Is Key

Stay with the Nature

A park is beautiful. However, the less pristine and natural the place, the better. Take note of sounds, sights, and scents. Find 5 unusual things that can be used to tell people about the area and capture video or photos. Even if it's not your home, you can still search for the sky and see exactly what it looks like that day.

It's a good idea to get busy and also do some dirty work. It doesn't really matter what you do, because it can make your life easier. This strange effect is caused by M. vaccae microorganisms that get onto your skin. These microorganisms can trigger the body to produce more serotonin. This natural chemical can help boost your mood.

They will tell you if they say they are better than when they dig up dirt. Now, take off the horticulture gloves and start moving the dirt around.

Many sufferers of seasonal affective disorder, or SAD, experience dizziness during the months when there is little sunlight. Even if SAD isn't affecting you, it could affect your ability to see the sun. Take at least 15 minutes to go outside on a cold day. You can still walk fast, but also get some sunshine on your face. Vitamin D, which is often lacking in many people, can be created by the sunlight.

Recognize Anxiety and Uncertainty

Our sentences and the lies that we tell ourselves can create feelings of nervousness. The fear of being dissatisfied or lacking achievement. Fear of not being accepted and also the fear that others will acknowledge you. The fear that you will not be enough. The fear of being rejected. Are there lies or fears that are keeping you from moving forward? Although we all cannot go back to our old lives and start over, we can take the first step today to make another life. Today is the beginning for the rest your life. The past isn't the same as the future. We need to let it go and move on to the present. Start preparing for the present you want and also not accepting unremarkableness. If you stop doing the things that were making you overweight, then you can adjust. Recognize the fear of what you accept as legitimate versus what remains.

Take advantage of the bonus social

As an automatic tension-reliever, keep in contact with the person you value. Hugs, as well as holding hands with people that you trust, can be healing for both of your bodies. The Journal of Option and Corresponding Medicine conducted research that found massage therapy can boost your immune system and produce more product.

Massage therapy specialists can help you boost your body's immune system.

Consider treating yourself, even if you can't get a massage from a friend or loved-one.

If you are unable to supply others, discovering means that you can provide them with something. I have stopped speaking to someone and now offer my ears. Volunteer at a local charity or help a friend who is in dire need. You'll see your problems differently. Recognizing that you have the ability to make a difference in others' lives will help you feel much better about yourself.

Like a caring friendship, friendship needs nurturing. A friendship that is neglected will lead to a loss of a friend. You should see your friends as often you can, if it is convenient for your schedule. If you have a family, it is a good idea to meet up once per week for football or a TELEVISION recommendation program. For people without families, a month-tomonth dinner group might be a better option. You need strong relationships to overcome any obstacles in life.

Being socially active doesn't have to seem difficult. Look for methods to improve your relationships with others. Think about the activities you love and look into ways to share them with others. If gardening interests you, consider joining a nearby backyard. If you love to cook, please share your creations with your next-door neighbors or the community firehouse. The following are some other ways you can find joy with others and avoid isolation:

Offering

Finding a cause you are passionate about and volunteering your time to help it is one of the most rewarding ways to spend time. Volunteering at a local animal shelter or helping children in need can help you build connections with others from different generations. These connections may benefit from a fresh perspective or introduction.

Registering with a club and/or taking a course

Meet people who are interested in the same things as you, or take a class on something that interests you. Each of these jobs requires our mind to be involved in new ways.

Part-time jobs

Part-time work is a great way to make connections and make some extra cash. While it may be hard to get back into the workforce, you will find that this is a great way to meet new people as well as to develop new partnerships.

Why you must remain social

Brightened Spirits

Spending time with people you enjoy can boost your mood. The benefits of making connections with others are that we feel more involved in the world around and can reduce our anxiety.

Enhanced Physical Wellness

Friends are more likely to take part in activities that support our physical health than when we are alone. Being around people can also help us to achieve our goals of being healthy and balanced.

Boosted Immune System

The immune system performs better when people are actively involved in social activities. This shows that socializing can help to keep immune-harming bugs like the flu away.

Sharpened Mind

Social jobs offer mental work and exhilaration, which can help improve memory function and cognitive function. A happy mind can help you avoid or slow down the progression of Alzheimer's disease.

Good sleep is essential

Social isolation can cause anxiety and anxiety, which can then lead to flustered evenings. Research has revealed that those in fulfilling relationships are more likely than others to be able to relax as well as feel freshened.

Concentrate on the positive.

To find long-lasting joy, it is important to change your negative mental frame to one that is positive. You can try these things: Spend 1 to 2 minutes looking for positives in your daily life. You can do this 3 times per day for 45-days, and your mind will start to do the same. You can choose a good rule to follow for the day, something you can easily duplicate like "Today's attractive" or "I am grateful for all that I have." If things get difficult, try to see the situation from a positive angle. Never underestimate the importance to acknowledge the silver linings of life.

Commemorate little victories.

Although life can be full of ups or downs there is always some small success. Let's take a moment to recognize this little success. Did you get all items checked off on your order for business that you have been putting off. Yay! Did you not delete a thousand spam emails from your inbox last week? Woohoo! You will get a kick from this little success. They add up!

You can find your balance between your job and your personal life.

While work occupies much of our time, it is not the only thing we should do. It is crucial to seek out passions as well as jobs. Do you have hobbies? Are you socializing with other people as well as your loved ones? Are you working out? Finding balance in your life will reduce stress and anxiety. It will also provide you with other electrical outlets that can be used to have fun and expose yourself.

Method mindfulness.

Mindfulness arbitration jobs require you to bring your acknowledgment and also interests to the present minute. It's about accepting your feelings and also being non-judgmental. Mindfulness means being present, mindful, curious, and open to change. Accepting the situation we find ourselves in reduces anxiety and stress. This helps us to see possibilities of what they might be. Mindfulness allows us to find peace within ourselves and also affirmation.

Use your creativity.

While musicians might be considered moody and depressed, there are studies that show that regular participation in imaginative activities can actually make you more happy. People who use their creativity and are creative often feel more fulfilled and happier. You can create, attract, or paint these innovative tasks.

Accept the problem.

There are many of us who strive for excellence. We prefer to push ourselves to the limit. You must be okay with the imperfections of life in order to truly feel satisfied. Quality is not easy. In addition, holding others accountable for our needs is futile. You will experience pull-downs all the time. Recognize the fact that life isn't perfect, and that imperfection can lead to beauty and elegance.

Do what you are passionate about.

It's difficult to find happiness when you dislike your work. Even if you're making a living, don't let your best years go to work that isn't fulfilling your needs. What are you thinking? What is your passion? Do a structured occupation in an inspiring area. It will provide you with high levels of satisfaction and help you to increase your happiness.

Chapter 8: The Basics Behind Self-Sabotage

Nobody would ever think of sabotaging themselves. Although it sounds funny, it is actually quite common. We don't realize it because it's all happening subconsciously. Your subconscious and conscious voices battle inside your head non-stop. That voice inside of your head, gnawing at you and telling you to quit is a familiar one. Sometimes you believe it, and then give up. It's the thing that keeps you from living your life to the fullest. It's a defensive mechanism designed to prevent you from making mistakes and failing. The downside is that it doesn't allow us to take on risk.

Self-sabotage involves a lot of negative thoughts that try to keep you down. While you may find yourself criticizing yourself for past errors, remember to always be gentle with yourself. The key to seeing yourself outside of yourself is to see you as someone else. This helps you to see the situation objectively and gives you an opportunity to find new ways of looking at it.

This article will show you how to overcome the destructive patterns of behavior that are keeping you down and make you miserable.

1. Understanding how to identify maladaptive patterns in behavior.

2. They can be overcome by increasing motivation, will, and self-actualization.

Mindfulness

Self-sabotage can be made possible by neglecting your emotions, needs, or desires. We are more likely than others to be self-destructive and self-demeaning if we avoid getting to know ourselves. This is the essence mindfulness.

What can we say about someone who is conscious? You can describe it as a fourth dimension. Everything is subjective, so words are not the best way to describe it.

We can however say that it is an awareness and attention on purpose in the moment. It does not require judgments. This allows you to be more self aware, self-knowing, sagacious.

Kabat Zinn stated, "We all take ourselves very seriously because we consider ourselves to be the center of life." This story about "me", which features me having interactions with other humans, is the way many people perceive life. This process makes it difficult to see the truth. We were all presented with a range of choices at one point and then we chose what we believed was the best.

So, we start to question our own self-worth.

Are you your name

Is it your age?

Do you have thoughts?

Are you even your genetic inheritance?

Are you familiar the narrative voice that follows your every move, opinion, judgment? This is the point of the old saying, "The questions we asked are more important that the answers we came up with."

These brilliant words by Kabat Zinn were accompanied with mindfulness techniques. This will allow you to move away from your "me", and instead focus on the part that isn't there.

Breathscape practice for cultivating mindfulness

This one is complicated and requires multiple steps.

1. Take control of your posture.

2. Recognize that the information you're about read is the same information you already have. The present moment should be experienced in silence, with someone saying it to and even if this is your first

time reading it. This text will serve only to guide you into your inner world.

3. When you are done with all the distractions from your internal world, take a deep breath, and reflect on your true aspirations and ambitions.

You should also remember to keep your body fully relaxed, and to pay attention to your breathing. As the most vivid sensation in the moment, picture your breath. Feel the flow of air in your body from your nostrils to your belly.

Allow the breath to flow naturally. Let your attention and focus be on the breath you're doing now. Don't hurry the process. Let it flow as it is intended. If you find it takes you some time to digest everything, then take it slow and do not rush.

1. Take a look at your wandering thoughts and you will notice a pattern and a life. It is possible for a thought to pass while your attention is on the breath. This gives you evidence that it isn't me and has a way

with its own thoughts. You might be anticipating events or recalling past events. Or maybe you are having an argument with yourself about a subject. It won't bother you if you just keep your eyes on the breath and let it go.

2. Be open-hearted and kind to your thoughts. If the center of attention is not in the breathing, then what?

3. Relax and focus on your breath again. Repeat all steps necessary to create a steady, natural flow of air.

4. As you imagine yourself being on various types of breath waves, thoughts may appear again. You can openly examine them, and you'll be able to see what thoughts are coming back at you.

5. Accept this entire process as an act to show kindness and love to yourself, just the connection of your breath.

6. You can be alert now, slow and steady, without any other agenda. The new, fresh

air is a new beginning. As you breathe, your sensations will change. After letting go of the stoic posture, you can now embrace each breath.

Depressive people simply believe that they are bad. I don't have any value. Others see my insecurity. I don't need to speak up for myself. Others will see how insecure I feel." These are some of the core beliefs that many people with depression hold about themselves. These beliefs are usually too negative, pessimistic, or distant from the truth. Nobody is perfect. But depressives believe such things and continue to reinforce their negative hypotheses. In order to prove their worthlessness and their success, depressive individuals will try to set the bar too high. Failure to meet their goals will make them more depressed, pessimistic or negative. If they follow the so-called "SMART" goals, it will be easier to end their self-sabotage.

1. Specific- Instead saying "I want" or being the best, one should be more specific. Specific goals, such as "I want a university degree" or "I want the ability to play my favorite music", are better.

2. Measurable "SMART", or measurable, goals are easy to measure. "I want to be successful" is more difficult to measure. Measurable goals, on the other side, have an objective scale so it's easy to identify success or failure. Depressive people can also be affected by goals that are difficult or impossible to measure.

3. Attainable: We need to choose goals that are easily achievable. Keep in mind that while these goals shouldn't be easy, they should pose a challenge. The key word here is balance.

4. Realistic - These goals need to be achievable and can be applied to real-world issues. It is one thing to learn Greek. But, it is important to think about how this

would impact your quality of life and overall skills.

5. It is important to have time-bound goals. This will ensure that you don't self-sabotage. Be careful when setting due dates. It is important to be realistic as rigid due dates can discourage you. Breaking a few unrealistic due dates will lead to you abandoning them completely, which is always bad.

Chapter 9: Calming Your Mind

You are correct if you believed that this blog was going to be all about meditation. Meditation was bound to be here. It's a powerful tool.

An online seller friend introduced me meditation. When I complained about how stressful it was for me to have a full-time job and run my business in the night, he explained to me that he meditates daily and it helps him to relax and stay focused on his daily tasks.

Prior to that I had never considered meditation. I know the benefits are there, but it wasn't something I thought was worthwhile. I would rather just lie down and drift off to sleep. Personally, I would prefer to go for a nap.

I was experiencing a lot stress. My journey to become a successful businessman began when I took an online selling class.

I had always dreamed of owning a car lot. But, I realized that such a venture requires significant capital.

Also, I didn't have any idea about running a business. I know how to sell. Sales are what make the money. I knew that employees needed to be paid but that was it.

I had to learn everything I could about business if I was going to be a businessman. Shark Tank was only recently launched, and I felt it was a good place for me to start.

One thing led another and eventually I was able to sell on Amazon.

The learning curve was steep because at first I didn't need a computer. I was familiar with how to use computers and I even had one. But I mostly used my computer for entertainment.

It was also quite different to what I was used. Selling cars to people involved talking to them and persuading them with your words.

You aren't always speaking when selling online. Instead, you write. Even though you can sell online via video, it is still not the same as selling face-to–face.

Instead, it was necessary to use specific data sets in order to discern what sales are good and which ones don't.

I also had to keep track my inventory, supplies, as well as taxes.

I was a drug sales rep back then. My drug rep friends thought it was crazy. At the time, that was how it looked. I wasn't making any big achievements, only a few hundred extra for groceries.

I had also spent significant money to obtain relevant online courses as well as to buy inventory. I was also spending late nights ordering and shipping stuff.

I will admit it, I thought I was crazy for doing this back then.

However, I still had something in my heart and this was just the beginning. It was something I wanted to do because it allowed me to learn. And in that regard, it was quite successful. I gained a lot from that experience.

It was also very stressful.

After I finished my homework, I watched courses and did research. Then, I ordered supplies, packaged products, and drove them to the Post Office the next morning on my way home for my first appointment.

I was feeling overwhelmed and began to consider getting meds to help me.

When my friend recommended that I meditate, I was eager to do it.

I learned from a simple Google search that I should simply be in a comfortable position and close my eyes. Then, focus on maintaining my breathing.

To be completely honest, I thought it was rubbish. It's basically trying get to sleep but not letting you fall asleep.

But I was desperate. This is all I've tried so far, except to see my doctor and get some meds.

It turned out that the first time I did it, instead of taking a rest, I actually took a nap. It was so monotonous that I just went to sleep.

I tried again the next evening. It was very good. It was amazing. I could do it for a few seconds and was calm and relaxed. I loved it.

I think constantly, right from the moment I wake-up, to the moment just before I go to sleep, and every moment in between.

I was taking classes each night to learn business concepts, and was constantly traveling and meeting new doctors and pharmacists throughout my day.

I was also trying my best to contact suppliers and order shipping and handling on the way to each destination.

As you can see I am constantly on the move and my mind is always working.

It was getting to be too much. I was developing a mild anxiety disorder. Because my brain is always on overdrive, I started to feel doubtful. I began to think of different scenarios and imagine future possibilities.

Remember, I was a successful salesman. Although I wasn't the most popular and confident boy in high school, I feel enough confidence in my abilities to approach anyone.

Additionally, my experience in the workplace has taught me how I can talk to people about nearly any topic.

My mind was simple. I knew what needed to be done and I did it.

The fact that I suddenly had four to five different ideas at once was starting to confuse me.

I've never been afraid of embarrassing myself, but I started to worry about how to approach the doctor. I was trying predict what might happen because I was constantly thinking about possible scenarios.

The information I gained about the business had a profound effect on my thinking. My side-business is beginning to influence my job.

After finishing my hour with the courses, I tried to reach out to suppliers from India or China. I was researching on products to see which ones I should be selling. I was looking at ways to save money and optimize my business process.

All this requires that you can quickly shift your focus to make lots of decisions and implement many things.

I've always worked in a variety of jobs, but I was a hard worker. I talk to people and try to negotiate with them.

My experience in the illegal substance market could be considered running an enterprise, but it's different from actual, legitimate businesses.

I was very busy and my mind was in overdrive. I knew I had to do something and I had to get it done quickly. Otherwise, it can spill over into my family life.

It was already something I had experienced, so I decided that meditation would be a good option for me.

Even though it was for a brief time, feeling calm and clear in my head was a great feeling. Also, it felt amazing to release all the tension in my body.

I decided that I should keep practicing. I thought I'd be able to keep doing it for longer if i kept practicing.

I was also thinking of adding a simple step from a book I've read. I wish I could find it so I could give the appropriate recognition.

The first step was to imagine that I was in a room of empty white with paper with writing all over it. Each piece was a thought. The room was my brain.

I would then take out all of the paper pieces and clean up the trash bin. The trash container disappears.

It has helped me tremendously. It is something that I continue to do. It's part of my meditation ritual.

Once I have settled down and closed my eyes, I picture the scenario. I can then visualize the scenario almost instantly after I am done.

This is really all that I do -- it's just me, sitting in comfort and releasing stress every night for about half an hour.

It's not possible to give you any information about meditation that you don't already have access to online. That's where meditation was first learned to me.

It does work, I can assure you.

You don't need to be guided. All you have to do is get into a comfortable posture, close your eyes, focus on your breathing, and then relax.

You can let go of your thoughts.

Relax and let go of all your worries.

This is not to say meditation isn't relaxing for me. I simply enjoy having half an hour a day without worrying about anything.

It's like having a little break from everyday life. It has also made me more open-minded and relaxed. I was able to manage my thoughts better and stopped worrying about unnecessary and unimportant things.

Meditation could be described as giving me more control of my thoughts.

It makes sense, because you are controlling your mind during meditation and not letting other things bother you.

I'm not an expert in meditation so please don't quote. But, for me, the most important thing about meditation is not how you feel during meditation. It is the practice of controlling your thoughts that is the real benefit.

While meditation is helpful for those who practice it, it doesn't solve the actual problems. However, the mind training that you do when you meditate is the foundation to what you need in order to hack your brain.

Meditation is an excellent way to enhance your brain and learn to control it.

This isn't because of the meditative experience, which is a tremendous benefit in itself. It is more about the ability to control your thoughts and place them where you want them to be.

This ability is useful in mind hacking as it helps you organize your thoughts to create structures that will help you make improvements over time.

It is likely you have developed bad habits over the years that you have been unsuccessfully trying to change. Perhaps you feel frustrated at the fact that you keep trying to make progress but never seeing any results.

Mind hacking works. But it only works if done correctly.

You'll be disappointed if your mind thinks it can just rebuild your brain overnight, and then become a completely different person the next day.

It just doesn't work that way.

They estimate that it takes more than two weeks for a behavioral habit to become a normal behavior. Depending on how long you've been practicing the habit, it can take a substantial amount of time to break the habit.

I am sorry that you wanted an instant solution that would work in an hour, but that isn't the case.

Mind hacking works in the same manner as regular computer hacking. While you can accomplish amazing things with it it takes some effort.

As an exercise, I'd like to encourage you start meditating if this is your first time.

I would suggest that you stop reading this book and instead focus on learning how to do meditation. Everything in this book will draw upon the knowledge you have gained from meditation.

Just find a peaceful, secure place. For fifteen minutes, set a timer.

While it is only for a very brief period of time, I want to encourage you to stay there without falling asleep.

Meditation is a great way to relax and fall asleep.

Begin with fifteen minutes. If that's not enough, you can go on to thirty. However, make sure you don't fall asleep.

You can then relax, take a deep breath, and begin to clear your thoughts.

While you can use the same technique as me with the papers or the trash bins, it's not necessary. You are free to come up with your own methods, provided you know how to empty your mind.

You're done.

Alternativly, you can either focus on your breath or a single thought.

You need to learn to put your thoughts aside for a while and not be distracted for more than a few minutes. When you're able do this, and can stay there for at least fifteen mins, you should feel ready.

If you can do the job for longer periods of time, it is obviously better.

As you become more familiar with the process and get better at it you'll be able work faster and accomplish more tasks in a shorter time.

You can start by meditation. Meditation can help you calm your mind, and take the worries out of your active thoughts. Learn to control what thoughts you are thinking and where to put them.

You'll be able at the very minimum to control the thoughts and keep space in your mind. In the next chapter, you'll learn about the benefits and how you can prioritize your thoughts. All you have to do is learn how to do this at will.

Chapter 10: Self-Sabotage And Sexuality

Every person deserves a fulfilling, healthy relationship with their partner. Like food and drink, sexuality is a natural part our lives. Even though we're not necessarily dying for the act of sex, from a superordinate perspective our species would be an endangered one without it. Because of this, sex is very important to us.

Things are not always the same in all households. However, nothing is exciting or the things that everyone secretly hopes for. Many people have learned how to deal with their situations. They don't talk about it, and they don't find solutions that work. Additionally, there are many blocking beliefs that we have in our heads.

We are descendants of post-war generations and the war. We now face rape and our husbands who lost their lives or were wounded in combat because of the horrors that our grandparents and fathers went through. These women were forced to either make their own decisions or deal with their husbands returning home from war. They were never the same men they married before. There was not enough space to express one's feelings. The luxury of thinking about oneself or the relationship was not available. It was all about functioning and survival.

Therefore, our grandparents and parents weren't great at explaining and modeling feelings and relationships to our children. Relationships and marriages back then lasted longer than they do today. However, this doesn't necessarily mean they were happier. In such circumstances, the physical body was more a source of shame than pleasure.

These are some examples of common phrases or dogmas that still have a positive effect today.

Sexuality serves reproduction only – Sexuality has no importance – Sexuality does not provide fulfillment – Sexuality is not about pleasure - You can't have what you want You must be strong and suppress your feelings of weakness. What matters is achievement. Love is just an additional - Each man for himself! - People can be bad. – You must keep up. – The body functions. - You cannot leave your partner.

Even though it has been a long time since we were sexualized, many still hold sex as a taboo. For some, it's an irritating part of daily life that we have incorporated into our lives because it somehow belongs. We are constantly under pressure because there is almost no commercial or film that doesn't have a sexual component.

In terms of sexuality, we've never been more free than we are now. But we don't have the freedom to do so in a more autonomous way. This overgrown freedom comes with a drawback, which is often ignored. It is our strongest drive or impulse, no matter what we think.

I encourage you to ask the following questions.

Do you want a fulfilling sex lifestyle? Are you even sure what that means? Do you even know what your desires are? Are you content with what is available? Are you aware of your belief system/dogmas? Are you able to give the best of yourself and others what you desire? Are you still not fulfilled? Are you on a quest to find your true purpose?

I want to congratulate those who live an amazing sex lifestyle that fulfills all your needs and makes you feel happy. Enjoy it.

Or did you find myself asking questions that made you ponder and caused you some anxiety? Are you feeling something is off? This program can help you restore things that have been in a rut for too long.

It is okay. It's okay for things quickly to change and run smoothly. It is important to remember that you don't have to be under any pressure. You don't have the right to conform to what is expected of you.

Sexuality is just as individual as any other human being. Our sexuality is unique because there are no two individuals exactly the same.

There are no rules or guidelines that everyone must follow. It is up to you to discover your own truth, and to decide how to handle this problem. For a happy sex experience, it's all about releasing your inner demons.

Some people consider sex unimportant and don't use it. That's o.k. That's as long as they are not forced to suppress their own wants and needs. There are solutions for every kind of relationship. Many times, it is our beliefs patterns that stop us searching for a shared pathway.

Carl has been married for over 25 years to Irene and they have three kids. Their family appears happy from the outside. Everyone, even their closest friends, knows that Carl has been suffering for around twenty years. Irene has never shown any appetite and Irene has always refused to go to sex. Irene is also refusing to attend the couple-therapy Carl recommended because she did not want anyone to hear about their private struggles. Carl gave up on the marriage and started cheating with his wife five years earlier. They never talked about it. Both of them suffer. Carl longs for a meaningful relationship rather than his secret sexual encounters. Irene is scared of losing her husband, their family idyll.

Carl holds these beliefs:

*,,You must not leave your wife."

* *„I am not allowed to get the things I want."

*„I might only experience secretly the things I desire."

These patterns are shared by Irene.

*„Sexuality only works for reproduction. Surrender is dangerous.

* You must not expose your weaknesses. Your strength is what you need to make an impact.

*„In our families women are strong, while men are weak; losing power is a sign to weakness, and therefore frightening."

Carl is unable move beyond his subconscious blocks to solve his problem. I don't believe it is a wise idea to divorce your spouse. However, if Carl is not willing to make significant changes and continue working on the problem together for a longer time, then this might be the last resort. They must find another outlet if both partners are unable to stop their inner turmoil.

Irene has deep beliefs that she is unable to give in to her feminine and sexual nature. She has little sexual drive and desire. As long as the outside appearance is more important to her than the inner, she will continue to hurt herself and her husband. But the belief system that hinders sexuality being fulfilled does not necessarily have to do directly. The perception of

*„Life is hard"

Problems in this area could also result. Why? Because sex shouldn't be serious, but fun. If you live a difficult and challenging life, this is not possible. The inner conviction

* "To be loved, I must conform"

You stop living authentically and instead try to satisfy others' needs. You do what your partner wants, but they don't serve you. You know the expression

*,,I'm just not enough"

Because you are insecure or always doubting yourself, it can prevent you from allowing for physical love.

Sabotage in sexuality can lead to us choosing partners who don't allow us to live a fulfilled sexlife. People who have no luster or demand practices that we don't enjoy, criticize or are just not available to us attract us. Potency problems or denial, no desire or desire - these are all signs that obstructive thoughts patterns have created possible blocks.

There's also self-punishment through recurring infected because you might feel deep down that your sexuality may be illegal.

Sexuality is about flowing. If you don't allow life itself and happiness to flow, then you limit your ability to experience all of the physical world.

This book will reveal your hidden beliefs system. Once you finish it, you will be free to change any situation, open up to the possibility of releasing yourself, and accept the flow of your physicality. It is part you and perfectly normal.

First, you must allow sexuality to be part of your daily life. Next, experiment with it and learn how it works.

Chapter 11: Low Self-Esteem

The Problem

Self-hatred isn't a pretty sight but it is something we see more frequently than we would like. Many people don't have self-esteem. They aren't able to see their uniqueness and appreciate it. Many people engage in self-sabotage by using all manner of means to degrade themselves. Because they don't believe that they are entitled to it, they can actually cause damage to the relationships of those around them.

It may be difficult to accept that you fall into this category. However, if you do recognize the pattern in your behavior, you should pay attention to it and seek to create better feelings within yourself. Low self-esteem can cause serious problems in your life. It can make you miserable and could hinder your happiness.

Keep in mind that you are not the only one suffering from low self-esteem. It can seriously harm your chances of success and cause other people to feel the same. Your potential for success in your professional and personal life is being missed if you continually underestimate your capabilities and value. Your low self-esteem prevents you from being the go getter you need to become and fighting for the things you want and deserve.

Think approximately how many chances for development you've exceeded or what number of enjoyable relationships you can have constructed with notable humans, but you haven't, because of your low shallowness. It is actively negative, it encourages self-sabotaging conduct and it desires to stop. There's a completely real chance of it becoming a vicious circle in which you skip up opportunities, due to the fact you discovered you're not accurate sufficient after which your conceitedness drops even more, preventing you from taking advantage of the following possibility.

Surely you could see how this may emerge as a one-manner charge ticket to Crazy Town, so you need to agree that you need to take some time to place a save you to it. But how will you acquire that? Continue studying and you'll discover.

The Solution

You don't have to stay your entire lifestyles being managed through your loss of conceitedness. You can in truth take rate and alternate topics for the better, however first, you need to really want to. You need to agree with that there's extra to it than meets the attention and that you may beautify your lifestyles and prevent sabotaging yourself, whether or not or now not or now not you apprehend it or now not. In order to gain this, you will should begin strolling on building up your conceitedness. Yes, this is some thing you may do and you will research the way:

Surround your self with positivity

I'm not constantly speakme about international-peace, make-love-now not-warfare shape of positivity, but injecting a dose of positivity in your each day life, mainly with reference to your self, your person and your competencies. For example, a extraordinary exercise you may attempt is to inform yourself some detail awesome every unmarried morning.

Every day, when you awaken, I need you to face inside the the front of a reflect and tell your self a few factor appropriate approximately yourself, a few thing high nice, some aspect precise or some factor you apprehend about yourself. This receives you used to hearing and accepting high-quality mind and phrases and slowly, however genuinely, you will start appreciating them and believing them.

You furthermore want to ensure to pick out your friends cautiously. You don't have any use for individuals who are constantly seeking to supply you down. Negativity will now not assist you in any manner, so spending time with someone with a terrible thoughts-set will absolutely undo any improvement you could make. Instead, keep out with satisfied, cheery, effective folks that usually remind you techniques incredible you're and apprehend your many inclinations. The environment may be very crucial in the way we recognize ourselves and having an super set of pals and family who love and help you is beneficial to the technique of studying to like your self.

Make a list of functions

Continuing on the preceding idea, each different effective problem you can do is make a list of all your inclinations and strong elements. Take some time to sit down down with a bit of paper and a pen and genuinely don't forget the whole lot that is sincerely amazing about you – the big subjects and the little subjects. Every little detail counts, because it's a new danger that lets in you to discover ways to admire your capabilities.

At first, seeing this list of traits which you respect also can revel in overseas to you and you may surprise who this individual is, due to the fact they sound incredible on paper. But at the identical time because the fact of who you are will begin to sink in, it's going to be the maximum extremely good, eye-starting up 2nd within the worldwide, agree with me. Open your mind and your coronary heart (and your ears!) and absolutely pay attention to what others have to say suitable about you and what you be aware collectively with your private eyes on that piece of paper. You are plenty greater than you're inclined to comprehend and if you brilliant gave your self a chance, you will see you're no longer as lousy as you believe you studied you are.

Keep track of all your successes

Similarly, you may probable want to place down each fulfillment you've ever head. Again, they'll be huge ones or small, normal ones; it doesn't depend, because of the fact they'll be all crucial. You need to learn how to respect your self for the whole lot you do and from each element of view. So, permit's say you write "Completing my Bachelor's Degree"; you're additionally going to jot down "Rescued a kitten from a tree" or "Made genuinely proper paella". Every accomplishment is treasured and they all contribute to the development of your conceitedness.

Looking at an prolonged list of successes is clearly one-of-a-kind than genuinely thinking about them. By writing them down on paper, you are faced with them straight away, and also you cannot deny what's on that listing. You are consequently compelled to truely take delivery of that you are an high-quality individual, which you are sensible, capable and precious as an person and as a person.

All of those wearing activities will assist you exchange your mentality completely. It gained't seem in a unmarried day, that's proper, but there's no doubt that you may begin to see the fact peeking from under all the ones years of misery and self-doubt. At the forestall of the day, your goal is to begin accepting your self, appreciating what you have to provide and loving yourself for who you're. Only whilst you start this adventure will you be capable of prevent conducting self-sabotage and begin growing a higher lifestyles for your self.

Chapter 12: Increasing Productivity

Self manage and could power are each underneath your manage. You can modify them as in step with your dreams and continually aim at maximizing them on your advantage. We checked out the subjects that you may do to increase yourself manage and will energy within the preceding chapters, respectively, and in this one, we are able to study at the subjects that you could do to boom your normal capacity and productiveness in lifestyles.

Say certain more

The golden rule of growing your productiveness is to say positive greater. When you are saying certain, no longer satisfactory will it inspire you to take in difficult obligations but additionally let you push your limits. Regardless of whether or not or no longer it's miles a project at domestic like walking errands or a venture that your boss goals you to complete, the extra quantity of sure that you deliver away, the extra the blessings a wonderful way to come back your manner. So don't expect times in advance than giving some aspect a nod, mainly if you think you're capable of doing it. Some people may have a superiority complicated and chorus from agreeing to some thing actually because they desire to show off their authority. But doing so will only purpose your self control and will strength to bog down and so, it's miles high-quality that you permit glide of your ego as an entire lot as feasible to see fantastic progress.

Get rid of distractions

When it entails increasing your productiveness, ensure which you get rid of all types of distractions. Distractions can't virtually waste it sluggish but furthermore deliver down your stage of productiveness to a totally huge quantity. Whether it's far a person or a trouble this is distracting you, make sure you do no longer supply into it and excellent consciousness on finishing your responsibilities first. To help treatment this case, you could set apart a bit time to take pride on your distractions on a every day basis. Dedicate half-hour to an hour and do the entirety which you count on will otherwise distract you on the same time as you are performing some issue essential. This can be chatting, messaging, taking issue in social media, looking something and so on. Once you sense satisfied, you could now not have the urge to have interaction in them whilst you are doing a little element important.

Set a timer

Setting a timer is a superb manner to increase your productiveness. Whether at art work or in any other case; set a timer and try to finish the project within the set time. Just be cautious to not rush into something because it is able to now not will let you obtain preferred consequences. For example: if you have to do the dishes, then set an alarm and try to finish it inner that point. It is exquisite that you have the alarm in sight as you will be able to music your development. Once you word which you are nearly finished and there may be nonetheless some time left, you can come right into a further enthusiasm and end up quicker. You can appoint comparable techniques everywhere which incorporates your artwork vicinity. You will satisfactory get more paintings completed and it will will can help you growth your common productivity.

Prioritize

When at paintings or some different location, you want to prioritize the whole lot that you do. If you observed a effective difficulty will reason you to have behind schedule effects then make certain you do not have interaction inside the ones sports until you have had been given attained preferred consequences. For instance: in case you suppose attending a useless assembly will handiest cause you dispose of with some thing that you are doing, then you may in truth ask permission to bypass it and preserve doing all your undertaking and finish it early to build up better consequences. Similarly, if there is a possibility to bypass some detail a high-quality way to maintain doing some thing that you are doing, then it's miles awesome which you undergo in mind that alternative.

Break

The human frame calls for relaxation sometimes. When you overwork, your productivity will surely turn out to be low. To help remedy this problem, you have to take normal breaks out of your paintings. These breaks need to be of types. The first kind being the mini breaks which you take inside the route of the day that will help you loosen up and rewind and the second type being taking a holiday or taking location a vacation to help you harm away from the monotony. Both the ones will flow a long manner in helping you growth your productivity and achieving larger and faster outcomes. Chapter 5 explains strategies in which you may take a damage throughout your art work hours to help you get returned to doing what you are while no longer having to sense burdened or over worked.

Early to bed early to upward push

Productivity and sleep patterns have a proper away connection. When you desire to increase your productivity, you need to acquire as a minimum 8 hours of undisturbed sleep. And this sleep desires to be ideally early night to early morning sleep and so that you need to cause at hitting the bed at 9 and getting up via using 6. This will no longer certainly make certain which you get your due rest however additionally make sure you have got enough of day time on your fingers to do all your duties. Try to schedule your existence in the sort of way that you are completed with the whole lot through eight which includes dinner. This will help you meet your nine pm last date and assist your frame avail the due rest that it merits. You can lease an alarm clock to wake you up within the morning so you can kick begin our day on an early have a look at.

Don't watch TV

The tv is thought to purpose human beings to experience a reduction in their diploma of productivity. Mainly, thinking about that it could be a distraction and more importantly, because of the truth it's going to cause human beings's brains to gradual all the manner all the way down to a very huge quantity. When you watch TV, you'll now not be capable of remember something and as an opportunity have to take delivery of everything this is being proven to you. So in desire to dropping time looking what extraordinary humans need you to assume, you could alternatively spend the same time analyzing a unique or an high-quality ebook and help increase your understanding base. There is a method called conscious studying, it is defined in the subsequent financial ruin and you may make better use of the expertise which you benefit.

Know to outsource

Outsourcing is a wonderful concept because it will help you garner large and higher results. Say you need to kind 500 sheets of some thing and the faster you do it, the extra cash which you make. You can lease 10 people and get the project completed quicker and are to be had right proper into a earnings after paying anything is because of them. Similarly, you may outsource all your artwork anyplace which you are consisting of having a person to help you with chores across the house, delegating artwork at your industrial enterprise and so on. Don't assume outsourcing will make others query your productiveness and actually, it'll superb purpose them to just accept as actual along with your judgment and choice making capacity.

Speak about your dreams

It is belief that speakme up approximately your dreams lets in in developing your level of productivity. If you preserve your dreams to your self then it couldn't encourage you to install your top notch. What you may as a substitute do is to inform your family or some of your pals approximately your goals and this could inspire you to pursue it better. You also can write it down and stick it inner your material cloth cabinet, place it internal your desk and so on. This will help you maintain the diverse goals in sight and allow them to live to your thoughts for longer. Once you understand your goals, you could enjoy inspired to preserve this manner going and it's going to nice increase your degree of productivity.

Bonding

It is thought that bonding higher with the humans spherical you'll growth productiveness. So if you have to artwork with a team at workplace, bonding with the contributors will help you growth your productiveness. If you bond at the side of your classmates, then you can carry out properly at university and lots of others. You can also have a form of emotional and highbrow resource system in play on the way to allow you to artwork properly. You will discover which you are able to paintings faster within the enterprise agency of people that you are snug with and not fearful of being judged. If you want to transfer a employer then try to befriend your colleagues as fast as viable to help you start operating at a higher tempo. The equal applies to gelling collectively at the side of your boss as you could have the freedom to paintings for your non-public area and now not sense pressured.

These shape the severa strategies wherein you can decorate your productiveness and make the extremely good use of your intellectual and bodily capabilities.

Chapter 13: Persistence Promotes Progress

I need to tell you a story approximately staying strength and religion. The story is ready the Chinese bamboo tree. This story is one of the tremendous examples of the manner staying strength can pay off and the manner building a robust basis is essential to fulfillment.

When the bamboo tree is planted the farmer waters it and nurtures the plant for a whole developing season. Every specific plant begins offevolved to sprout and shoot thru the soil subsequently of this time, however now not the bamboo tree. After all the mild love and care the farmer gives to the plant no longer whatever appears to be the cease end result, however the farmer maintains to water the plant and fertilize the soil. Another growing season passes and regardless of all of the farmers efforts the bamboo plant although has no longer sprouted. Even but the farmer keeps to water the plant and fertilize the soil. He continues to nurture the plant for 4 years at once. In 4 years this plant apparently has now not grown at all! The farmer has typically watered and fertilized the plant and however not something has came about.

The 5th three hundred and sixty five days rolls spherical and miraculously the bamboo tree grows eighty-90 FEET in 6 weeks!!! That's eighty-ninety ft in a single growing season. Although it regarded similar to the tree wasn't developing the least bit, it turn out to be clearly developing a robust and notable root system. It become making prepared itself to preserve the tree. The bamboo tree developed a robust basis so that after it modified into established it may reap its whole capability. It can also have appeared that the bamboo tree become a slow starter in assessment to exceptional timber and flowers that sprouted before it did, but the bamboo tree ultimately grew taller and stronger. The farmer who planted the seed had key dispositions that have been vital and critical to the tree's success, staying strength and religion.

This is the correct equal method we ought to expand thru, pun supposed. Lessons may be discovered from the farmer and the tree. The farmer teaches us a way to have patience and keep religion. Had the farmer dug the seed up in disbelief the plant would possibly grow, stopped watering and nurturing the plant due to the truth he didn't see any improvement, he might have destroyed the tree. Because of the farmer's faith he persisted and nurtured the tree. Because of his staying strength the tree developed efficiently resulting within the business enterprise basis which allowed for the 80-ninety toes of increase.

The tree teaches the significance of growing a company foundation. Had the tree not superior a robust basis it'd were not feasible for the tree to maintain the boom on the same time as it sprouted. Without the ones strong roots the bamboo tree may not be capable of get the water and vitamins it dreams and will blow away with the wind. How many human beings do you understand that start a "change" in their lives and the primary impediment that they come closer to it's like each of their hopes and dreams are demolished? They didn't have that man or woman nor endurance that could allow them to take that hit and keep going. There have become no foundation!!! This is one important purpose why building your beliefs of who you are is so vital. You can be so superior that even if worrying situations do upward thrust up you're able to conquer them and keep attention at the reason.

We have the splendid responsibility of being the farmer. We plant the seed (paradigm) in our minds and it's as masses as us to have the religion which lets in us to remain affected person and persistent. We have to constantly nurture our ideals which can be normal with that seed. Even if you don't bodily see what's taking area. That seed will develop the roots it wishes to be sturdy and appear the bodily that you can see. Those roots (thoughts) must branch out for more nutrients from the care you've given it. This is also building individual. You will become stronger and stronger as someone. Once you have got had been given that strong foundation you will begin to see that your inner global absolutely does create your outer international.

Tips to Empower Yourself

During this journey you may have times in which you feel like not anything is taking vicinity. It happens! Don't panic, don't' doubt, don't stress about it. Continue to increase your self. Remember that you need to BE so you can purpose you to DO and result in the HAVE.

Affirmations and Declarations

One manner I improve my ideals is through doing affirmations and declarations. Affirmations are terms that you could use to embed a advantageous notion of your desire into your unconscious mind. Declarations are statements that you say that assist a brand new perception. I generally repeat my affirmations and declarations every day and multiple times. Why? Because individual are creatures of dependancy. When we again and again do advantageous topics we begin to create that dependancy. This is why the right repetition is so key to fulfillment. The affirmations and declarations inspire you. They placed you in a first-class state in an effort to make more potent the center beliefs you need to have. For example; some of my affirmations are

1. The Creators wealth is circulating in my existence. His wealth flows to me in

avalanches of abundance. All of my needs, goals, and goals are met right away. I am one with the Creator (taken from Tony Robbins)

2. I am so happy and grateful now that money flows to me in increasing portions thru a couple of assets on a non-forestall foundation. (taken from Bob Proctor)

3. I can also have a successful day due to the fact I am a a achievement individual.

4. I now command my unconscious thoughts to carry me the humans, events, instances, the self guarantee, and statistics anything it takes for me to close my enterprise corporation gives.

five. I in reality have all I want interior me.

6. I commit myself to reap my goals

7. I end what I begin

8. I will only choose out out mind and emotions that guide my happiness and success

I truly have affirmations for each factor of my life my fitness, rate variety, relationships, personal development, and corporations. I say these sayings out loud and make certain I add emotion to every saying. I may snap my fingers, clap my palms, or possibly leap up with joy. I create a strong emotion alongside component every saying. This places me in a top country of notion and truth. I get charged up and I enjoy splendid!! Another awesome aspect I do is I voice file myself saying my affirmations and repeating my dreams as if I've already finished them. I take note of the recording at the equal time as I'm laying down at night time time and even as I'm dozing. Why?

Do you know that at the same time as you pay attention exceptional human beings inform you, you may do it, you're the extraordinary, you're a success and so forth., it best resonates a piece? However, when you pay attention yourself say it, you believe it! When you pay attention yourself repeat some problem constantly it begins offevolved to replay in your mind. You will discover that little voice beginning to change. Instead of these terrible mind of "no you may't, don't even attempt, why even hassle… you'll concentrate the sayings you've repeated. Yes I can, I am the pleasant, I am a achievement, I'm a extraordinary lover, I'm pleasant for this possibility, and so on. Even if the little voice gives you a tough time and has a few difficulty poor to say. You'll observe yourself preventing the mind and deciding on to handiest accept as true with what helps your success. Recording your self pronouncing your affirmations and desires will help to embed those ideals into your mind as it's YOUR VOICE!

Canceling Unwanted Thoughts

Now notwithstanding all of those techniques every so often the unwanted thoughts though pop up. I recognize that when I actually have an concept or scenario that plays in my head that I don't accept as genuine with in I simply say Cancel! I snap my fingers and say CANCEL! CANCEL! CANCEL!! And I right now popularity on what I want to occur in my life. Or if I discover myself reliving beyond reminiscences that weren't right, perhaps an argument or so, I've skilled myself to trap it. I say CANCEL! That's in the beyond. I can best impact my destiny. I then ask myself what do I need to look from this place of my existence within the destiny and I begin to attention on that alternatively.

www.ingramcontent.com/pod-product-compliance
Lightning Source LLC
Chambersburg PA
CBHW060237030426
42335CB00014B/1501